The Natural Path

From Nature, With Love

An Introduction to Soapmaking

Instructions & Recipes for All-Natural Living

Willa Daniels

Willa Daniels

An Introduction to Soapmaking

Willa Daniels

The Natural Path
An Introduction to Soapmaking
Copyright © 2024 by Willa Daniels

First Edition: October 2024
This edition was first published in 2024

Cover design: Serenity Endeavor Press
Editor: Monica Bogza, Trusted Accomplice

ISBN: 978-1-961501-04-1 (Paperback)
ISBN: 978-1-961501-05-8 (eBook)

Printed in the United States of America
Published by: Serenity Endeavor Press
https://jenflanaganbooks.com/

Willa Daniels

Table of Contents:

8>8">888

Willa Daniels

Basic Soap Recipe & Instructions **29**

Luxurious Spa Soap **39**

Calendula & Marshmallow-Root Soap **42**

Sea-Salt Soap **45**

Laundry Soap **47**

Bubble Bar **49**

Charcoal Detox Soap **51**

Goat Milk Soap **53**

Mix-Ins **56**

Mint **57**

Honey Oat **58**

Sea Spa **58**

Lavender **58**

Grapefruit Ginger **58**

Coffee Addict **58**

Natural Sponges **59**

Natural Colorants **60**

Mix-Ins for color **60**

Water infusions **61**

Oil Infusions **63**

Troubleshooting **64**

Overflows **64**

Liquid Center **65**

Weeping or Oozing **65**

Cracks **65**

Crumbles **65**

8

Willa Daniels

To all those who are trying to live a little closer to the earth, for whatever that means to you. My hat goes off to you.

I hope you have fun experimenting with these recipes.

Willa Daniels

Overview

All the recipes in this book can be made in your own home, with natural, biodegradable, non-toxic ingredients. Most can be found at your local health-food store.

However, if you don't have one nearby, you can easily find them online. I use Amazon for a lot of my ingredients, as I can get them in bulk.

I will provide easy, step-by-step instructions with pictures wherever necessary.

These soaps are perfectly safe for sensitive skin, kiddos, or washing pets, too. Just be careful of the scents you use. Cinnamon smells great but can be irritating and abrasive to the skin. It's fine to use a small amount with a fall-scent mix, but go easy. Use your best judgment.

After using our own bar of soap for a couple of years, I find that my skin is so much more nourished and that regular soap irritates and dries it out. We have extra soap bars and hand soaps in travel containers when we are away for any length of time.

Because these soaps are non-drying and have a nice lather, they also make great shaving soaps. I haven't used shaving cream in years. My husband even uses the Calendula soap for shaving with a safety razor.

Measuring and safety are of the utmost importance! This is chemistry, folks. Deviations can cause the soap to not properly set up or the pH to be too high, which can result in caustic burns. Make sure to use all recommended safety wear and caution. Don't deviate from the weighted measurements.

Congratulations on starting down The Natural Path!

What Brings You Here

You may want to remove toxins and chemicals from your life. Maybe you want to save some money or try homesteading. You may be a crafter and want to create something fun for your family or *with* your family. To all the above, I say great. Welcome!

I've met people with skin issues who can use nothing but these soaps because they contain only the most simple, non-abrasive ingredients.

Customization

I will suggest herbs or essential oils to add to the soap. Some of these are to soften the skin or to help with the cleansing power of the soap. Sometimes, they are just to make it smell good.

Feel free to substitute whatever scent or herbs you choose. If you want to use a fragrance oil, go for it. Just make sure you keep it within the weight measurement.

You'll notice I don't add as much scent as allowed. My soaps are lightly scented. This is partially because essential oils are expensive, and I personally choose not to use scent oils in soaps. I've provided the maximum scent you can add to each recipe. Feel free to increase the amount up to the maximum if you want to achieve more fragrance.

I've included a section with ideas for mix-ins, my favorite mixes, and ideas for natural colorants. Have fun experimenting. Just be careful not to add things that will change the chemistry, like added sugars (think milk, fruit juice/purees), unless you research it a bit first.

My recipes will fill a 3-pound, rectangular, standard soap mold, but you can use anything from a Pringles can to SOLO cups, a bread-loaf pan, or fun silicone molds purchased online. If you go for a loaf pan, you'll need to line it with parchment paper, letting it hang well over the sides to help with the removal. Pringles cans, SOLO cups, or Styrofoam will have to be torn off the soap when un-molding, making them single use. This is a great way to upcycle any you might have on hand.

If you're adding honey or going into the gel phase, you won't want SOLO cups or Styrofoam as these containers could melt in the extreme heat.

Shaped cutters can be used for texture, although I typically use a chef's knife.

The recipes I include tend to make medium-hard bars of soap for longer use. They use easier-to-find and cheaper oils that aim to cleanse without over stripping and have a nice lather.

There are several soap calculators out there, but the one below is my favorite. You can play around with the different oils and qualities (hardness, cleansing, bubbliness, creaminess) based on the types of fatty acids in the oils or fats you choose.

The calculator will tell you how much lye, water, and fragrance to add for the selected options. This is a great way to take soapmaking to the next level.

http://www.soapcalc.net/calc/SoapCalcWP.asp

Note: I'm not affiliated with soapcalc.net in any way. I just really appreciate their calculator.

Reducing Chemicals

It's very important to me to have low chemical exposure. Skin is our largest organ and it protects our body. I want to nourish it with natural products that support its elasticity, tone, and health.

I also want to reduce the amount of chemicals used in the community. Crafting your own products also reduces the amount of waste in the world. Every little bit helps.

Some of the scents I use are not 100% natural. The product is still natural. Just the customized scent choice is not. I only have a few scent mixes that aren't 100% natural.

My personal view is, if I can get my kids to use a natural product with no known toxins, it's still less chemicals than they were previously using.

It's all about a good balance. Honestly, unless you're willing to carry a small container of liquid hand soap or a bar of soap around with you anytime you leave your house, you're not going to be able to get rid of 100% of chemical exposure to your skin. Soap in our workplace and in the local stores where we shop at often contain questionable ingredients.

Feel free to stick closely to my recipes or play with colorants or scents as you see fit.

Safety

Please exercise safety while making soap. If you involve your kiddos, make sure they are old enough to do the work, understand the safety concerns, and use safety wear. A great idea would be to have them help scent or color the bars, or simply to help pick out the scents and colors.

Always wear gloves while making soap. Because lye has a very high pH, it can burn the skin. You don't always feel this burn when it happens because it is an alkali, a caustic base.

When mixing it into water, measure the water and lye separately, then slowly add the lye to the water, so it doesn't splash out. Only do this in a well-ventilated area, or preferably outside, as it does generate some fumes.

Have vinegar with the lid open on the counter, ready to use. Any kind is fine but white vinegar is the cheapest. It is acidic and instantly neutralizes the base. In case of a spill, pour vinegar over the exposed skin or counters to neutralize it.

Protective eyewear and an apron are strongly encouraged, especially as you get started.

Wash your dishes in warm water while wearing gloves. After washing everything, rinse with vinegar water (50/50), then re-rinse with water or re-wash as desired.

What Is Saponification?

Soap is made from a reaction of lye and fats. You need enough fat to saponify the lye. Saponification is the conversion of fat or oil into soap through a reaction with an alkali.

Traditionally, castile soap was made exclusively of olive oil because it was made in the Castile region in Spain (hello, olives). Today, it denotes any vegetable-based soap (free from animal fats or synthetic ingredients).

I'm not opposed to using animal fats myself, but I've never tried it. Depending on your own personal preference, feel free to explore the soap calculator for different vegetable oils, butters, animal fats, and waxes.

I'd love to hear how it turns out!

Superfatting

No, I'm not talking about the ultimate anti-diet. I'm talking about soap. *This is a soapmaking booklet, after all.*

Superfatting counteracts the cleansing attributes, acting like a buffer to prevent over stripping. Any percentage of fats in the recipe exceeding those able to saponify in the lye-water solution is considered the superfat percentage.

I personally would never superfat less than 5% for a body soap, due to discrepancies in scales and how well we measure and scrape out containers. This provides a little safety measure to ensure the proper resulting pH of the soap.

Most of the time, I prefer to superfat by 5-10%, to moisturize or counteract a high-cleansing soap. The higher the superfat, the softer the soap and the quicker it dissolves with use. I have had soaps not set properly when I went up past 15%.

Coconut oil would need to be superfatted higher to counteract its extremely high cleansing attribute. **The superfatting percentage doesn't change the amount of oil or water used, only the amount of lye used.**

If you're using unstable oils, like unsaturated fatty acids, you don't want to go over 7% superfatting as they could go rancid. All oils used here are saturated fatty acids. Each recipe has the superfat percentage noted.

The Challenge

I realize it's easier to pick these products up at the local big-box store. You will likely spend more money, but you will definitely save time. Don't let the amount of time, energy, or safety measures discourage you.

I challenge you to pick a recipe to start with. Read through it first, so you can get the ingredients you need and understand the process. Make sure you have everything weighed out and ready, including all safety precautions, *before* you start.

I make soap bars once a year. It takes 2-3 hours on a Saturday. I make two double batches, resulting in four 3-pound molds.

Make it fun. Get your kids involved! My daughter likes to customize her own scents in her soap and has a slightly different recipe for her preferred bar. She likes it extra bubbly.

Remember, it's about progress, not perfection. Any step you take toward natural is a win. Take it.

Ingredients

Lye

NaOH, also known as sodium hydroxide, lye, or caustic soda, is a white, inorganic, ionic solid compound generally found as granules.

It's an alkali (base) and highly caustic, decomposing proteins at ordinary ambient temperatures, which causes severe chemical burns if you're not careful.

Cue the gloves. Wear them, friends.

Sodium hydroxide, lye, has a pH of 14, the highest alkaline on the pH scale. When saponified, cold-process soap is naturally alkaline with a pH of around 9-10 to gently clean the skin.

You should be able to find lye in any garden or hardware store or online. Food grade lye has fewer impurities and has less trace metals than technical grade. I've heard that there's no way to prevent any metals, and some soapers use the cheaper technical grade with no issues. I've only used food grade but use what works for your budget.

Keep it out of the reach of children and only open it when wearing gloves and over a solid surface. Granules tend to scatter.

Coconut Oil

Coconut oil, whether virgin or refined, has a melting point of 76 degrees Fahrenheit. If it's been hydrogenated, it melts at 96 degrees. I use the 76-degree version. The refined coconut oil is much cheaper, scentless, and perfectly acceptable if you're not trying to add in the qualities of the coconut oil. Use whichever works for you.

You can always use unrefined coconut oil in a body butter to enjoy its skin-nourishing qualities.

Coconut-oil soap produces a nice, hard bar, with bubbly qualities, and is high cleansing because of its ability to grab oils.

Fractionated coconut oil doesn't have the same fatty acids and cannot be used as a substitute. If you want to use this, you will need a soap calculator to find the correct values, but you will find it is extremely hard and stripping, with no conditioning qualities at all.

In winter, this oil is hard. I bring it in from my garage to warm it up, but it only has to raise above 76 degrees to melt and be easy to pour, or to the low 70s to be soft enough to spoon out to measure. Setting it close to my stove or heater a day before making a new batch of soaps generally takes care of it.

Never melt it in the microwave or boil this oil. Heat gently in a double boiler if necessary.

Make sure your oil is pure, with no additives. Any additions can change the chemistry. Check the ingredients.

Olive Oil

There's no need to use extra-virgin olive oil; the cheaper stuff is fine. Just make sure it's pure olive oil. There are a lot of mixes out there. Read your labels.

Olive oil is high in conditioning attributes and inexpensive but results in a softer soap.

Castor Oil

Castor oil is highly conditioning, bubbly, and creamy, but makes a soft soap with very little cleansing capability. It's great to add to other soaps to improve the lather.

Castor oil is more expensive, but you typically won't use much of it, and it comes in 2-oz containers.

Palm Oil

A lot of soapers use organic palm shortening in place of palm oil. I personally do, even though some soapers have concerns about it not being the same. Its acidic makeup is similar enough to palm oil to use it as a substitute. I've never had bad results.

Palm shortening is a natural source of vitamins A, C, and E and has antioxidant properties. It's so high in vitamins that it's used to treat eczema, acne, and dermatitis.

Palm oil is medium high on conditioning and creaminess, but not as bubbly. It's lower in cleansing, so you'd want to combine it with a higher cleanser. Often, these conditioning and creamy oils drastically reduce the hardness. Palm oil, however, maintains a decent hardness.

Shea Butter

You will want only unrefined, raw shea butter. It comes in yellow or white versions, but both colors are the same quality.

This ingredient may be harder to find, but I add shea butter to only one recipe as a nice option. It is highly conditioning and creamy, but it doesn't mean a softer soap.

It is, however, lower on cleansing attributes, so it's nice to add a smaller amount as a conditioner with creamy lather to coconut-oil soap, as it maintains the harder, longer-lasting bar. It can be a more expensive option for this conditioning quality.

Colloidal Oats

You can easily make colloidal oats with a small coffee or spice grinder. Simply grind rolled oats very fine, and voilà!

Avenacin is an antifungal and antimicrobial constituent found in oats (avena sativa). They have saponins, which help cleanse, and flavonoids, which might help absorb ultraviolet-A rays. Other benefits come from their vitamin E, which is anti-inflammatory, along with phenols and starches to help in moisturizing.

Oats are known for their ability to treat eczema and poison ivy irritation. Grinding them to a fine powder allows them to be even more effective at protecting and soothing.

Clay

Clay is a natural detoxifier that has a very nice and smooth texture. Add this to your bar of soap for a spa-like soap experience. Because of its absorbent properties, it's used in beauty treatments to draw out impurities and toxins from the skin. It's also used to tone and firm, while stimulating the circulation, and to tighten the pores, exfoliate, and heal blemishes.

Bentonite clay is made from volcanic ash, most of which is produced in Wyoming, USA. It's used to add a nice slippery texture in soaps (think for shaving) and high absorption (think to remove toxins and acne).

Green clay (illite) has a finer texture and lots of lovely minerals for your skin, such as magnesium, calcium, potassium, zinc, silicon, selenium, iron, copper, and cobalt. They also include iron oxides and can contain decomposed plant material, such as kelp and seaweed, giving it a green hue. It's often referred to as French clay because the rock quarries in the South of France yield most of the world's illite deposits.

Kaolin clay is a very fine powdered clay and comes in a variety of colors, which makes for a fun, natural coloring of the soap. It's often used in eye shadows and cosmetics and is a little less liquid-absorbing than most.

These are just a few clays that are easier to find, but feel free to research and explore other options and colors.

Because of the mineral content in clays, you shouldn't use metal to measure or store them. The minerals could cause a chemical reaction like oxidization or rust. A small wooden spoon works. I eyeball the measurement of this mix-in as it's not crucial to the soap's success.

You can mix clay with witch hazel or apple cider vinegar for a great detox mask (face, armpits, or feet) or to pull out other impurities, like splinters!

Honey

Raw honey is incredible for your skin due to its antibacterial properties and antioxidants. This makes it not only a great treatment for acne, but also for aging. It's a humectant (moisturizing), soothing, and opens pores for cleansing.

You might not get as much benefit from it in soap as you would applying it as a mask, but it still packs a mighty punch. It also increases the lather in your soap.

Sugar causes soaps to heat up (as do milk and fruit), which can cause the soap to go through a gel phase if it gets hot enough. A gel phase is when it heats up to 180 degrees and can result in brighter colors and a shinier appearance.

Unless you are aiming for gelled soap, I would avoid it as half-gelled soap can have cracks on the surface and a deeper color at its center like a raw center of dough in a loaf of bread. Or it could spill out of the mold entirely onto your counter.

I've done it myself, friends. Check out the photo in the Troubleshooting section if you'd like to see.

It might not be as visually pretty, but once it's aged and the pH level is stable, it's perfectly fine to use. Or chunk it up and add some into future bars.

I find that using a maximum of 1 tsp per pound, so 1 Tbsp honey per 3-pound batch of soap, reduces the amount of gelling, leaving no cracks, and improves the moisturizing qualities of the soap. It also adds a nice caramel color.

Try these variations with caution, a little at a time. Please try this outside. The sugar could cause the lye to boil over if you're adding too much.

If your goal is to have more honey in your soap, try adding it to the water in the beginning and freeze it in cubes. Some people sprinkle the lye on the cubes and stir, adding more lye as you go until the honey water has melted.

I prefer to dissolve the lye into a smaller amount of water, like 100g, and add the honey water cubes to this, a little at a time to reach the full water weight. I've had good results doing it this way. Just make sure your oils aren't overly hot, as it does reduce the overall temperature of the lye.

Lowering the beginning point of the water keeps the lye from heating the mixture as much as it goes through this superheating process earlier on. You can also refrigerate the finished soap for 48 hours to reduce the risk of superheating.

Lavender

One of my favorite herbs, lavender, is used widely by herbalists due to its deodorizing, antioxidant, and disinfecting qualities.

Lavender is also used to heal cuts and burns, improve sleep, support brain function, relieve pain, eliminate nervous tension, enhance blood circulation, and treat respiratory problems.

The Latin name is Lavare, meaning "to wash."

I use it because of how calming and relaxing it is, and I especially love its deodorizing qualities (think running shoes and pet beds).

Also, it's one of the few essential oils that can be used neat, which means without dilution, without irritation.

Mint

Antimicrobial, mint is also cooling and calming. It improves mental focus and clears the respiratory tracts, which can reduce headaches and boost energy.

It's also used as an insect repellent, a sunburn relief, an anti-itch, and a fever reducer (cooling and calming, remember)?

Rosemary

Used as a respiratory aid, antiseptic, and antimicrobial herb, Rosemary is a good choice for bad breath, eczema, dermatitis (think dandruff and dry scalp), and acne. It's also energizing and stimulates brain activity, so it can help with depression, mental fatigue, forgetfulness, stress relief, pain relief, and headaches (especially those associated with muscle and respiratory pain).

Rosemary also aids with digestion, cramps, constipation and bloating, boosts your immune system, improves urinary-tract health, and stimulates hair growth.

Calendula

Sometimes called pot marigold or English marigold, these flowers aren't the same as the common marigold (genus Tagetes). Calendula has edible petals, unlike Tagetes marigolds.

Calendula is great for the skin, with benefits such as antifungal, anti-inflammatory, and antibacterial, which are useful in healing wounds, soothing eczema, and relieving diaper rashes. It's also a great antiseptic and often found in ointments, creams, and salves.

Containing flavonoids and linoleic acid, which helps fight inflammation, it's also been found to fight cancer and ease muscle spasms. In my opinion, its biggest benefit is in wound healing, by stimulating tissue and collagen production. I keep it on hand for my skin-healing salves.

Marshmallow Root

Marshmallow root contains mucilage, a slippery solution, which can be used when infused. This demulcent (cooling, soothing) quality means it's great for your digestion, skin, or hair. It's a soothing tea for sore throats!

It reduces inflammation (yay, for pain reduction) and speeds the healing process, which makes it a great addition to salves as well, healing eczema and soothing the skin.

Recipes

Basic Soap Recipe & Instructions

This is a good, easy soap recipe that you can customize with colorants, scents, and mix-ins for texture. It's just olive oil and coconut oil, resulting in a product that's fairly cheap to make.

Straight coconut-oil soap will give you a very hard, cleansing bar, but it's nice and bubbly. Olive-oil bars are softer, but nice and conditioning. This mix is 2-parts olive oil, 1-part coconut oil. Simple and easy.

I encourage you to start with this recipe because of the dual-oil simplicity, and it lets you skip any infusions on your first batch. Once you get the hang of it, you can get fancy-schmancy.

Make sure your coconut oil is soft enough to scoop prior to measuring. Get all your personal, protective, safety equipment out first and a vinegar bottle open on the counter. Measure out all ingredients first. ALWAYS weigh your ingredients. Warn your family that you'll be using lye and not to touch things without gloves. Put the dog out if he/she is a jumper.

Don't freak out. It seems scary, but once you do it, it's no sweat. Honest. One step at a time.

Recipe makes approx. 3 lb total weight (1.875 lb oils) and is 5% superfatted.

Ingredients
20 oz (566.99 g) olive oil (66.66%)
10 oz (283.49 g) 76-degree coconut oil (33.33%)
11.4 oz (323.18 g) water
4.31 oz (122.32 g) powdered lye
Up to 0.94 oz max (26.56 g) or 564 drops of essential oils/scent oils (optional)

Equipment
Immersion blender
Kitchen scale
Soap molds (approx. 3-lb (42-47oz) standard ones or a loaf pan (if using a loaf pan, line with parchment paper hanging over the edges to help unmolding))
Crock-Pot or stainless-steel pot to warm oils on the stove
Vinegar for safety and cleaning
Any mix-ins or colorants you choose (see the corresponding sections in this booklet)
Metal spoon
Spatula
Gloves
Apron
Eye goggles (optional)
Candy thermometer (optional)
pH strips (optional)

Directions
Measure oils, weighing them on the scale. Scrape the measuring container well with a spatula when pouring into your pot.

Warm oils. Setting temp to medium (Crock-Pot), or medium-low (stainless-steel pot), to gently warm the oils, but don't let them boil. They should reach approx. 110 degrees Fahrenheit. I don't personally check the temp, although some soapers swear by it.

Suit up. Put on gloves, an apron, and eye goggles. You look fancy. Pose for a photo op. Bonus points if you put your hair in pigtails.

Measure (and weigh!) the lye and water in separate glass-jars containers. Take them outside or to a well-ventilated area. Make sure no one will disturb the jars. I have a table out back where I know the dog can't reach, or I do this in my garage with the window open and let my family know I've got lye out.

Mix the lye and water. Slowly pour the lye into the water, not the other way around. This prevents splashing water up and out of the jar. Stir with a spoon, leaving the spoon in the jar. The jar will get *very* hot. Leave it to sit for about 10 minutes.

By this time, your oils should be nicely warmed and the lye is close to 110 degrees. Again, I don't measure, but feel free to. If you're measuring, the oils and lye water should both be around 95-115 degrees before mixing. This is ideal. They should be within 10 degrees of each other for easy processing and accuracy of reaching trace.
However, some people let them both cool to room temp before mixing the oils with the lye water. It's good that they're close to the same temperature.

Be careful your crockpot isn't too hot. Don't get impatient with solid oils and butters melting. Too hot oils will lead to overheating, gelling, and possible overflows.

Pour lye water into oils. Give a final stir of the lye water and slowly pour it into your oils. Set the lye glass and spoon in a sink or otherwise safe place for cleaning later.

Blend your soap to trace. Use your immersion blender to begin mixing the soap. It turns opaque almost immediately as it mixes, then thickens up and comes to trace.

Trace is when the mixture thickens to the consistency of pudding or mayonnaise.

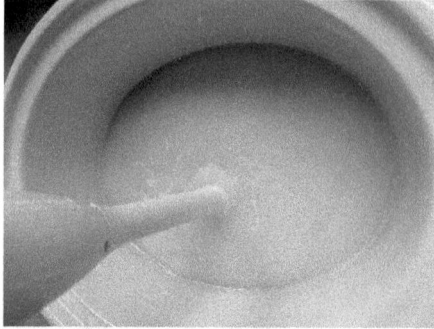

*Remember, this mixture is highly caustic, so don't touch it without gloves or splash it on anything. Keep your immersion blender in the soap while running, not letting it splash out. If anything splashes out, wipe it off with a paper towel and drizzle vinegar over it before washing it.

Follow either the cold or hot process as described below.

Cold Process

Once it reaches trace, **add in any mix-ins, colorants, or scents** you choose, blending or stirring with a spoon (or swirling it in) once more briefly to combine it. Colorants can be added earlier, at the lye stage as well. Don't overmix with the immersion blender or overcook at this stage. You're not hot processing it and you could get lumps of further cooked portions.

At this point, you are done and can **pour your glorious soap into molds.** Clean up and pat yourself on the back.... or make another batch, gently rinsing everything between batches (with your gloves on)!

Use the spatula to get all the soap out of the pot before starting a new batch or cleaning it.

Cold-process soaps will have a smoother top and will work with fancy molds much better than hot-process ones, which are firmer before molding. Results are smoother and prettier, better for swirling or layering soap. I also find that cold-process soaps retain scents better.

However, cold-process bars will have to set for 3-6 weeks before use. I strictly did the hot process for years because I'm impatient to use them. But now that I have stock and make many batches at a time, I use the cold process. It's faster to make multiple batches. See? Impatient.

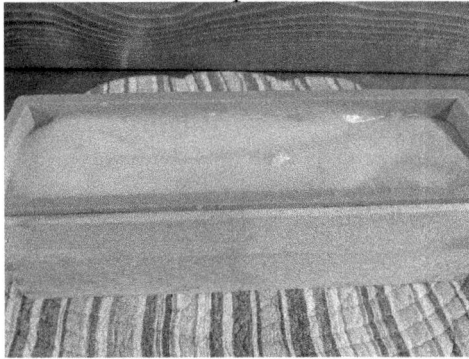

Hot Process
Put a lid on the Crock-Pot/soup pot. Make sure the temp is still medium to medium/low.

Let the soap cook for about 45 min to an hour, stirring with a spoon occasionally. Keep an eye on it. Don't let it get hot enough that it boils over. Slip your gloves off, putting your spoon in a safe place, and on while you're going about your day, cleaning the house, or enjoying a glass of wine/kombucha.

Store the immersion blender in a sink or a safe place to use later. I use a baking pan to store caustic supplies until I can clean them or an old cardboard box that I can throw away afterward.

The hot process allows the soap to completely go through the saponification process, heating it to speed it up. When it's finished, the soap is at a safe pH and can be used immediately after unmolding. Results are a natural-looking, lumpy-topped bar.

Stir every 10-15 minutes. The soap will come up the sides of the pan and fall in on itself. Don't let it spill out over the edge. An oily puddle will form in the center; this is extra lye that hasn't saponified. As it cooks, this will become smaller.

You'll know the soap is done when no, or very little, oily puddle forms in the center. The soap will be much thicker but will still stir. Feel free to use a pH strip to check the level. It should be around 9-10. I didn't use a pH strip for my first few batches. I let them sit a couple of weeks to be sure, and it all worked out fine.

Add in any mix-ins, colorants, or scents you choose, blending or stirring with a spoon again briefly to combine. It is harder to get them to completely mix at this point.

Spoon/pour into your soap mold. I recommend only using a loaf pan or plain silicone soap mold with hot process, as it doesn't mold as well into pretty shapes.

Scrape the sides of your pot with a spatula to get all the soap into the mold. Use the spatula to smooth the top of the soap or move it in a zigzag to make a pattern on top.

Unmolding
Let soaps sit 24-48 hours (for both the cold and hot process) in their molds. If using the cold process, remember to wear your gloves when unmolding as the soap is still saponifying and at a high pH.

Turn the soaps out of their molds. If using loaf-type molds, **cut them into slices**. I prefer thicker bars, over an inch thick. They break down much slower.

I use a chef's knife to cut it, as the soaps tend to be firm already. A wavy cutter makes fun shapes.

The harder the bar is, the quicker it firms up. If your soap is higher in coconut oil, you'll want to cut it right at the 24-hour mark, or it's hard to cut.

Hug yourself. You did it! You made soap! Queue the confetti.

Set the soaps to dry and harden on a cookie sheet or a parchment-lined counter to get better air flow. Soaps will continue to harden as they sit. I have a shelf in my laundry room that stays lined in parchment paper. I keep all my soaps there to dry and wait for use. I write the name of each on masking tape next to the line of pretty soaps, so I know which is which, with the date.

Hot-process soaps can be used immediately, but I would still suggest waiting a week or two to let them dry out a bit more. This makes the soap last longer in the shower. But no worries. No one will judge you if you grab a bar prematurely. I know you're excited to use it!

Cold-process soaps need to sit for 3-6 weeks to fully saponify.

Cleaning
After soapmaking, it's important to take safety precautions even while cleaning. Keep those gloves on. Rinse everything, scrubbing them in warm, soapy water. This will dilute and get rid of the lye, but I always run a little vinegar water over my utensils after cleaning, then re-rinsing, just to be sure.

Remember to wash your gloves last. They're on your hands, so it's easy-peasy.

I have an extra Crock-Pot I picked up at Goodwill for $10, plus a large metal spoon and a cheap spatula. Initially, I kept separate mason jars, spoons, and spatulas just for soapmaking. But as I got the hang of it, I quit worrying about it as much. If you clean your tools well, they are safe to use outside of soapmaking.

I now use my regular Crock-Pot and the Goodwill Crock-Pot to make two batches at a time. I eventually bought two more soap molds for a total of 4, or 2 double, batches.

If you're soapmaking two days in a row, you can even measure out your oils and have them ready in the Crock-Pots for the next day. Your prior day's soap will be ready to unmold, and you can keep going!

*When making multiple batches, I don't always wash my immersion blender. If it's in a safe place and doesn't dry out too much, you can use it for a second and third batch. Same goes for the Crock-Pot. Just keep track of what has been in contact with lye and what hasn't.

Note: This also makes a great shaving soap. Goodbye shaving cream!

Luxurious Spa Soap

The basic soap is great because it has only two oils and it's cheap. But I wanted to try for a more luxurious soap that was maybe a little fussier, introducing new oils, but not incredibly expensive or difficult-to-find ones.

I made this soap focusing on more bubbles, lather, and conditioning, while maintaining a medium-firm bar with reasonable pricing.

Finally, I upped the superfat to 10% for an ultra-moisturizing lather bar that feels like I'm spoiling myself. Why not?

I also discounted the water from the typical 38% to 35% to make a harder bar because of the higher superfat content. This is water as a percentage of oil weight. It will dry faster as well. A harder bar simply lasts longer.

Water discounting also speeds up the saponification process with a higher heat. Ensure your soap molds are stored on a heat-safe surface.

Since it's a harder bar, due to the water discounting, you'll want to unmold it after 24 hours for sure (not waiting for 48 hours) and cut it immediately.

Recipe makes approx. 3 lb, is 10% superfatted, and has 35% water as a percentage of oil.

<u>Ingredients</u>
12.9 oz (365.71 g) 76-degree coconut oil (43%)
12 oz (340.19 g) olive oil (40%)
3 oz (85.05 g) castor oil (10%)
2.1 oz (59.53 g) shea butter (7%)
10.5 oz (297.67 r) water – plus a little extra
4.18 oz (118.45 g) powdered lye
½ cup rolled oats (optional)
¼ cup chamomile (optional)
1 Tbsp of honey (optional)
Up to 0.94 oz max (26.56 g) or 564 drops of essential oils/scent oils (optional)
Safety and soapmaking equipment from the Basic recipe.

<u>Directions</u>
Measure the oats and chamomile into a heat-safe container on the scale. Pour boiling water over them to reach a weight of 11.4 oz. Let this sit for 1-2 hours or overnight. Strain and compost all oat matter.

You want the thick oat cream that comes from the strainer as well but not the flecks of oats, so be careful when pressing out the moisture. Sometimes, I double strain the chamomile oat milk. This keeps the resulting bar's smoothness.

You can skip the chamomile oat milk and simply use water instead. Feel free to use oat milk from the store, but if you do, make sure it's 100% oat milk, with no additives or flavoring. Check your ingredients so there's only water and oats! Ensure you use only 10.5 oz to replace the water.

Follow the directions in the Basic recipe, replacing the water with the oat water. You will need to add a little extra water to bring it to 10.5 oz weight after straining.

Add 1 Tbsp of honey and essential oils at trace if using the cold process or right before molding if doing the hot process. Follow either the cold-process or hot-process instructions (in the Basic recipe) to finish your soap.

Scents
Scent as desired. My favorite blend for this bar is below.

Honey Vanilla Chamomile: 100 drops of vanilla essential oil, 200 drops of chamomile essential oil, 50 drops of cedarwood essential oil.

Calendula & Marshmallow-Root Soap

Right now, this is my favorite soap bar. It's a bit fussier, but a real winner in texture, with a slick, velvety feel and tight, little frothy bubbles. Calendula is a skin healer, and marshmallow root is a natural humectant, trapping moisture and creating a lovely texture.

I've also discounted the water as I did in the spa soap. Only use dried herbs. Fresh herbs have water content, which could delay the saponification process.

This soap requires hot-water and hot-oil infusions of the herbs, which makes it fussier, indeed. It also introduces palm oil. This oil is a bit harder to find, but I've heard you can use (and have used myself) pure palm shortening. Just make sure it's pure.

If the Basic soap is easy and the Spa soap is more luxurious, this Calendula soap is like your over-the-top-fancy friend who is always put together and brings the best homemade sourdough bread with jam from a local blackberry patch. It's not as heavily superfatted as the Spa one, but your skin will drink up this silky soap. It's an entirely different type of pampering.

Recipe makes approx. 3 lb, is 8% superfatted, and is 33% water as a percentage of oil.

Ingredients
13.8 oz (391.22 g) olive oil – plus extra (46%)
9 oz (255.15 g) 76-degree coconut oil – plus extra (30%)
6.6 oz (187.11 g) palm oil (22%)
0.60 oz (17.01 g) shea butter (2%)
9.9 oz (280.66 g) water – plus extra
4.17 oz (118.20 g) powdered lye
Up to 0.94 oz max (26.56 g) or 564 drops of essential oils/scent oils (optional)
1 cup calendula petals (divided between oils)
2/3 cup marshmallow root
Safety and soapmaking equipment from the Basic recipe

Directions
I prep these items the night before and let them steep until the next day.

Preheat oven to 200 degrees Fahrenheit.

Pour boiling water into a large heat-safe jar (quart-sized) on the scale and weigh to the appropriate amount of water. Add 1/3 cup of calendula. Cover and steep for a few hours or overnight.

Weigh the olive oil and coconut oil in separate heat-resistant bowls (I use Pyrex). Add 1/3 cup of marshmallow root and 1/3 cup of calendula to each bowl. Stir and set in the oven. Turn the oven off. Let it steep for a few hours or overnight.

You want separate bowls because some of the oil will strain out with the herbs and the measurement of olive and coconut oil need to be exact.

Strain the oils and water into separate jars/containers to weigh. Add extra olive oil or coconut oil or water to reach the required weight.

The oils will go into your Crock-Pot or stainless-steel pot. Add the remaining palm oil and shea butter, weighing carefully.

Suit up with safety gear (in the Basic recipe). Carefully add the lye to your calendula water in a well-ventilated place.

Follow the soapmaking directions in the Basic recipe to come to trace, then add the essential oils, following either the cold process or the hot process (in the Basic recipe) to finish your soap.

I generally fill my mold a little short with this batch (and cut the bars a bit thicker) and pour the remainder into ½ of an upcycled Styrofoam cup or a bit of a Pringles can.

These round molds make excellent shave pucks. Just place one in a round container, pottery, or mug. Wet a shaving brush and whisk up a nice frothy **shaving soap**.

Scents
Scent as desired. My favorite blend for this bar is below.

200 drops of calendula essential oil and 100 drops of neroli essential oil.

Sea-Salt Soap

This is one of my newer recipes and has quickly risen in fame within my friends-and-family circle. One friend asked for an entire loaf of this soap for Christmas. She got it wrapped up in bows.

It's much harder, with tight bubbles, due to the high coconut-oil content, with the other oils balancing the party. The salt adds lather and visual texture, but it blends into a silky texture.

Any sea salt will do, but don't use Epsom salts or dead-sea salts as the other minerals can react differently and not set up properly. Magnesium makes it gummy.

Even 10% (85 g) sea salt improves texture. Adding the full weight of the oils as sea salt does risk a crumbly bar, so cut soon after molding (around 6 hours after) or add less sea salt to reduce this.

Recipe makes approx. 3 lb and is 5% superfatted.

Ingredients
22.5 oz (637.86 g) 76-degree coconut oil (75%)
3 oz (85.05 g) olive oil (10%)
3 oz (85.05 g) palm oil (10%

1.5 oz (42.52 g) castor oil (5%)
11.4 oz (323.18 g) water
4.89 oz (138.64 g) powdered lye
Up to 30 oz (850.49 g) sea salt
Up to 0.94 oz max (26.56 g) or 564 drops of essential oils/scent oils (optional)
Safety and soapmaking equipment from the Basic recipe

Directions
Follow the directions in the Basic recipe. I wouldn't recommend hot processing this soap. It might get too crumbly.

Add the salt just before it reaches trace. This salt is thicker than normal. Tamp it down to make sure you don't have gaps in the soap.

This bar hardens faster than normal. Cut as soon as it's firm to the touch (about 6-12 hours).

Scents
Scent as desired. My favorite blend for this bar is below.

Rosemary Mint: 200 drops of mint, 100 drops of rosemary essential oil

Laundry Soap

This is the only soap recipe I have that is only 3% superfat. I use it for my laundry-soap recipe, and therefore, it doesn't need to be moisturizing. Its only purpose is to clean clothes, so it has higher cleansing qualities and less superfat.

Use it for pre-treating. It's a nice, firm bar and useful to rub into a stain. I use my laundry soap to moisten the stain and then scrub this bar of soap over the spot. With an old toothbrush I brush in small, circular motions until the stain is gone. It works like a magic wand.

Recipe makes approx. 3 lb and is 3% superfatted.

<u>Ingredients</u>
30 oz (850.49 g) 76-degree coconut oil (100%)
11.4 oz (323.18 g) water
5.33 oz (151.17 g) powdered lye
Up to 0.94 oz max (26.56 g) or 564 drops of essential oils/scent oils (optional)
Safety and soapmaking equipment from the Basic recipe

<u>Directions</u>

Follow the directions in the Basic recipe.

Scents
Scent as desired or not at all. Below are a few options to assist this cleaning powerhouse.

Rosemary Mint: 200 drops of mint, 100 drops of rosemary essential oil
Eucalyptus Mint: 200 drops of mint, 100 drops of eucalyptus essential oil
Juniper Tea Tree: 200 drops of juniper, 100 drops of rosemary essential oil
Lavender: 300 drops of lavender essential oil

*I typically scent with lavender essential oil.

Bubble Bar

My daughter named this bar. She came up with this recipe herself to find a bubbly lather. It has nice, big, soft bubbles that foam up easily.

I wanted to keep the coconut oil, since it's so highly cleansing and cheap, but my daughter wanted to use castor oil instead of olive oil for a bubbly lather and creamy consistency. Since castor oil is fairly soft, she decided on a 75/25 coconut oil to castor oil.

It's slightly less conditioning, so we upped the superfat to 15% for a super luxurious bar. The high superfat works because of the hardness of the coconut oil.

It's definitely bubbly and creamy, while maintaining a nice, firm bar. I think she did a great job with it.

Recipe makes approx. 3 lb and is 15% superfatted.

Ingredients
22.5 oz (637.86 g) 76-degree coconut oil (75%)
7.5 oz (212.62 g) castor oil (25%)

11.4 oz (323.18 g) water
4.32 oz (122.55 g) powdered lye
Up to 0.94 oz max (26.56 g) or 564 drops of essential oils/scent oils (optional)
½ cup hibiscus flowers (optional)
¼ cup chamomile flowers (optional)
¼ cup lavender buds and stems (optional)
Safety and soapmaking equipment from the Basic recipe

Directions
Measure the dried flowers into a heat-safe container on the scale. Pour boiling water over them to reach a weight of 11.4 oz. Let this sit for 3-4 hours or overnight. Strain and compost all flower matter.

Feel free to skip the hot-water infusion and simply use water.

Follow the directions in the Basic recipe, using the pink, scented water in place of the water. You will need to add a little extra water to bring it to the appropriate weight after straining. Follow either the cold process or the hot process to finish your soap.

Scents
Scent as desired. My daughter's favorite blend is below.

Lavender Chamomile: 200 drops of lavender essential oil and 100 drops of chamomile.

Charcoal Detox Soap

Clarifying and detoxifying, I made this soap to help fight acne.
The activated charcoal helps draw out toxins and heal the skin.
Bentonite clay is known for its detoxifying abilities. It's not
overly moisturizing, but maintains a little superfat to prevent
over-drying the skin.

The oils I used are good for acne, they don't clog pores, and the
medium-chain fatty acids in coconut oil have antimicrobial
properties. Any leftover oil is unlikely to lead to additional acne,
but will soothe the skin and prevent it from overcompensating
with additional oil.

This soap is great after a hard workout to battle sweat and
bacteria, but also as a great facial soap. I typically cut smaller
bars or rounds from Pringles cans for smaller facial soaps.
They're great for traveling.

Recipe makes approx. 3 lb and is 10% superfatted.

Ingredients
15 oz (425.24 g) 76-degree coconut oil (50%)
9 oz (455.15 g) olive oil (30%)
6 oz (170.1 g) castor oil (20%)

11.4 oz (323.18 g) water
4.26 oz (120.89 g) powdered lye
Up to 0.94 oz max (26.56 g) or 564 drops of essential oils/scent oils (optional)
2 Tbsp activated charcoal
1 Tbsp bentonite clay
Safety and soapmaking equipment from the Basic recipe

Directions
Follow the directions in the Basic recipe. Add the charcoal and bentonite clay at trace if doing the hot process and right before molding if you're using the cold process. Follow either the cold or hot process to finish your soap.

Scents
Scent as desired. My recommendation for a scent to boost the clarify and detox theme is below.

Acne-fighting and detoxifying blend: 100 drops of frankincense essential oil, 100 drops of patchouli essential oil, 75 drops of tea tree essential oil, 75 drops of rosemary essential oil, and 50 drops of chamomile essential oil.

Other good acne-fighting essential oils include lemongrass, lavender, calendula, yarrow, lemon balm, comfrey, and thyme.

Goat Milk Soap

Fats in goat milk affect the superfatting percentage. You could do the math with commercial goat milk, but I've just went with a lower superfatting of 7% and had no issues.

Goat milk is known for its moisturizing qualities. It's loaded with antioxidants, lactic acid, and selenium, helps with inflammation and repairs the skin barrier, which can help with premature aging. It's also less stripping to the skin.

All milks have additional sugar. If you're using nut milk, make sure it doesn't have any added preservatives. I use raw goat milk from a local farm.

To counteract the sugars, you could use the ice cube method I talk about in the honey section, but I prefer to mix the lye with a little water as stated below, then add the milk cubes as I go.

Goat milk can burn if you heat it too rapidly. If it burns, the soap will smell and turn brown, but the final product is still safe to use after it cures.

Recipe makes approx. 3 lb and is 7% superfatted.

Ingredients

13.5 oz (382.72 g) 76-degree coconut oil (45%)
10.5 oz (297.67 g) olive oil (35%)
6 oz (170.10 g) castor oil (20%)
11.4 oz (223.18 g) goat milk ice cubes
3.5 oz (100 g) water
4.34 oz (123.03 g) powdered lye
Up to 0.94 oz max (26.56 g) or 564 drops of essential oils/scent oils (optional)
¼ cup colloidal oats
1 Tbsp honey
Safety and soapmaking equipment from the Basic recipe

Directions
Follow the directions in the Basic recipe, except only mix 100 g of water with the full lye amount, stirring well. Once this has started to dissolve, slowly add the frozen goat milk piece by piece. Stir every few minutes until fully dissolved.

Try freezing the milk in a gallon-sized zip top bag and breaking off smaller chunks. When weighing your frozen milk, if you're a little short, add water or liquid milk to make up the weight.

Do this outside in case it heats up too quickly and boils over.

Add the colloidal oats and honey at trace. Follow either the cold or hot process to finish your soap.

Scents
Scent as desired. My favorite blend for this bar is below.

Honey Lavender: 400 drops of lavender essential oil.

Honey Cardamom: 400 drops of cardamom essential oil. 1 Tbl ground cardamom.

Honey Vanilla: 300 drops of vanilla essential oil and 100 drops of neroli essential oil.

Mix-Ins

There are so many options for mix-ins. I have a few tried-and-true that my family prefers, and most often, they like it simple, with just colloidal oats and clay only to maintain the creamy texture, or none at all for a slick, smooth bar. I personally prefer a smooth bar.

However, sometimes, I add in things like ground walnut hulls or espresso-bean powder or coffee grounds. These provide some color and a nice scrubby texture. But most importantly, they look fun.

If you want to up the ante, you can mix the soap in bowls and layer the colors and textures. You can even pour half the loaf, then sprinkle it heavily with a mix-in, and finish pouring the rest of the loaf for a dark line in the center. Or just sprinkle some on top (think espresso powder) for a pretty topping.

Even something like sprinkles or jimmies can add a fun accent. They will wash away in the water as they're pure sugar. I would only add these on top of the soap after mixing and pouring. Adding them as a mix-in at trace could overheat the soap (sugar), and they would just melt anyway, leaving colorful streaks. Try it at your own risk, but watch out for overheating.

Try cubing a few especially colorful bars, adding them to a lightly colored batch for a nice contrast. This is also a great way to use up leftover soap slivers. Chop them up and add them to another batch.

2-4 Tbsp of a mix-in per 3 lb batch works well. My favorites are colloidal oats, clay, espresso powder, coffee grounds, and powdered herbs, like mint.

Don't add more than 3 Tbsp of honey per 3 lb batch.

Below are my favorite mix-ins, but play around and come up with your own or adjust these to suit you.

Mint

Parsley-water infusion (see natural-colorants section) weighed to replace the water in the recipe.

Scent the entire batch with mint essential oil. Pour half of the scented soap into the mold(s) to fill the bottom (creating a light-green layer).

Sprinkle with ground parsley powder (darker-green line).

Mix 2 Tbsp green clay into the remaining half of the soap. Pour over the parsley powder (darker-green layer). You can use a knife to swirl it if desired.

Optional: Mix it all together instead of layering it, or just partially stir, leaving streaks.

Honey Oat

Add at trace: 2 Tbsp of honey, 4 Tbsp of colloidal oats, the contents of 2 chamomile tea bags (optionally grind it into a powder), 100 drops of vanilla essential oil, and 200 drops of chamomile essential oil.

Sea Spa

Add at trace: 4 Tbsp of green clay, 1 Tbsp of dried mint (optionally grind it into a powder), 200 drops of mint essential oils, and 150 drops of rosemary essential oils.

Lavender

Add at trace: 2 Tbsp of colloidal oats, 2 Tbsp of clay, 2 Tbsp of dried lavender buds, and 300 drops of lavender essential oil.

Grapefruit Ginger

Grapefruit-peel & ginger-root water infusion (see the natural-colorants section) weighed to replace the water in the recipe.

Add at trace: 4 Tbsp of ground grapefruit rind powder, 200 drops of ginger essential oil, and 150 drops of lemongrass.

Coffee Addict

Use strong coffee, weighed to replace the water in the recipe. At trace, separate the soaps into two glass containers, approximately 2/3 in one container and 1/3 in the second.

Mix 4 Tbsp of fresh coffee grounds to the larger portion (add 2 Tbsp of cocoa powder for mocha). Pour into a mold to fill half way (coffee layer).

Scent the second, smaller portion with 100 drops of vanilla essential oil and pour it over the first layer in your soap mold. Sprinkle some espresso powder, additional coffee grounds, or full coffee beans directly on top. The resultant bar will look like a layered latte with a light foam on top.

You can use water instead of coffee for a whiter-colored foam.

Optional: Mix it all together instead of layering it, or just partially stir it, leaving streaks.

Natural Sponges

Okay, so this is more of a pour-in than a mix-in, but I think it fits well here.

Push a natural sponge or loofah down inside a Pringles can. Fill the can with liquid soap to mold. To unmold, you'll have to peel the Pringles can off the mold. Cut the soap into thick 1 ½ inch slices. Each bar of soap will have a chunk of sponge inside, ready to scrub.

You can even thread some natural twine or hemp rope through a divot in the sponge, but you'll want to do this right after unmolding, while the soap is somewhat soft. Use a thick needle or chopstick. If the soap is especially hard, try using a screwdriver to make a hole.

Alternatively, you can precut the sponge and lay it inside muffin trays (silicone or stainless-steel only) or single-soap molds. Pre-thread your sponges inside the trays so that, when you pour your soap, it encases the sponge, but part of the rope is still exposed to hang it in the shower.

Natural Colorants

Coloring your soap is entirely optional. I don't color most of my soap at all, except for what comes with my chosen mix-ins. The oils themselves tend to make a white to light-yellow soap.

Sometimes, I want to add a little color. Let your creativity fly!

Mix-Ins for color

Honey and colloidal oats turn this into a light caramel color.

Walnut hulls or ground coffee adds specks of color.

Clays will add a natural, easy color to your soap. I typically use green clay.

Charcoal will add, you guessed it, a dark gray or black color to your soap.

Powdered herbs, like parsley (green), mint (green), beetroot (red brown), and yellow dock (pink) add a nice light color.

Note: Make sure what you're adding doesn't have a strong scent. I added some spirulina powder to the soap once. It's a beautiful bright-green powder, rich in minerals, but as it comes from seaweed, it smelled a bit like it as well. It was a little fishy for me, personally, but you might be okay if you like it or you use less. It might work well with sea salt for a salty-briny soap.

Water infusions

This is basically tea, folks. Infuse the water in your recipe with a natural herb or spice to pull out its color into the water.

Use plenty of herbs or spices to ensure lots of color, as they will dilute with the oils when you add them together. Continue to add more until you achieve the desired result.

Cover the herb or spice with boiling water (measured for the required water in the soap recipe) and let it sit to steep for an hour or overnight. Alternatively, you could bring the entire solution to a boil and simmer it over low for 20 minutes. Just make sure you have ample water.

Try ½ cup of fresh herb or ¼ cup of dried and ground herb per 2 cups of boiling water. Adjust as needed.

After the water cools, strain the herb or spice (compost!), and let the water cool completely before weighing again. You'll have to top it off with extra water to bring it back up to the required weight before mixing it with the lye.

Natural colorants tend to work better with cold-processed soap. The hot process can reduce the color.

My favorite water infusions:
Parsley – Nice light-green hue, but no scent, so you can add what you want
Basil – Purply-gray hue, nice, clean scent
Mint – Nice medium green, plus smells great
Hibiscus Flowers – Beautiful pink color, light flowery scent
Dandelion – Light yellow color
Turmeric – Golden orange/yellow
Iris Petals – Differing colors based on the color and amount of color in the petals.
Daylily petals – The dark red produces a purple hue.
Beet Powder – Earthy red
Yellow Dock Powder – Natural to neon pink!
Citrus Rinds – Light yellow (lemon) to orange (orange/tangerine) to rose color (grapefruit). The more oil, the more color.
Paprika – Earthy orange red
Cinnamon – Rich brown
Cocoa Powder – Chocolate brown, plus a nice scent
Activated Charcoal – Black, also detoxifies and is great for a facial bar
Espresso Powder / Coffee / Tea – Light to dark brown. The espresso adds more scent than the coffee.

These are just to get you thinking. There are websites and Facebook pages devoted to it. Feel free to experiment.

Oil Infusions

Alternatively, you can infuse your oils. Use the same method as in the Calendula-soap infusion.

I don't do this as often, though, because water is easier and quicker to infuse. However, if you are looking to pull out the maximum of herbal benefits or color, infusing both the oil and water would give the biggest punch.

Troubleshooting

As with any other skill, this takes trial and error to get right. Experiment in a safe space, preferably outdoors with old cardboard, gloves, and vinegar handy.

This can happen to even seasoned soapers. If I play around with something new or get lazy, it doesn't turn out as expected. It's pretty rare that you have to scrap a batch, though. Hang in there.

Overflows

If your soap overflows or boils over, this overheating is generally due to too much sugar being added (honey, milk, natural colorants containing sugar, a chemical reaction from another mix-in).

It could also be due to the oils being too hot when you're adding your lye mixture. This happens to me if I'm

Liquid Center

If your soap isn't set in the center when you cut it, you've probably superfatted your soap too much. This happened to me when I started too. I cut into a perfect looking bar and the center tube oozed out. The melty soap is unusable, as far as I know, but the outer edges are fine once they've cured. Consider cubing them up and adding them into another batch of soap.

Weeping or Oozing

Separation can also happen if you've had false trace. It looks like trace, but it hasn't truly emulsified. Let it sit for several seconds to see if it stays, up to thirty seconds. If it still looks thickened like pudding, then you're good!

This can also be from high humidity, or fragrant oils not mixing in or not doing well in soap.

Cracks

This generally happens when the soap is overheating and goes into the gel phase. It's fine to use after it's cured.

Crumbles

This tends to happen when you've added too much mix-ins, overcooked your soap, or underfatted your soap. It can also be due to too much water.

You can try rebatching it by grating or cutting up the soap and remelting it.

Irregular Texture

If your soap comes to trace too quickly and begins to cook before you have time to add in scents or mix-ins, it can get clumps that don't hold the color or look different when cut.

Solid oils sometimes come to trace faster, as does overheated oils. Consider turning down your crock pot or taking it off heat once it's melted to cool slightly before adding your lye.

Mix by hand if it comes to trace too quickly. This will help reduce the additional curing before you're ready to pour cold process soap.

Too much water discounting can lead to trace too quickly, as can some fragrance oils.

Conclusion

There are so many variations and options you can do when it comes to soapmaking. Just check out social media, and you'll find even more to keep you busy.

I've seen soap so beautiful that it looks like candy.

I hope you try your hand at soapmaking and keep playing with it for years to come. Don't be afraid to try different things. Learn from them. Try more things. Find out what you love.

Whatever you do, do it with nature and with love.

Willa Daniels

From the Author:

Thank you so much for reading this book. I very much enjoy figuring out ways to be more self-sufficient. My soapmaking journey expands on my herbalism love and joins it with my joy of learning.

Soaping is a fun craft. The result is clean, gentle soaps that are not only a joy to use but nourishing for the body

Author Bio:

Willa Daniels is a fictional character created by author Jen Flanagan, a certified herbalist living in the Pacific Northwest. If you're interested in hearing more about Willa's adventures with her friends, her newfound magical abilities, and finding love, check out *Saltwater Cures (Orca Cove Series Book One)*.

If you enjoyed this book, the nicest thing you can do is leave me a good review on Amazon, Goodreads, Bookbub, or anywhere you review books.

Connect with me online:
Website: **jenflanaganbooks.com**
Follow Willa on Amazon
Facebook: @jenflanaganbooks
Instagram: @jenflanagan_author
Bookbub: @willa_daniels

Please visit my blog at **jenflanaganbooks.com** for upcoming books, comments, and minor musings.

Willa Daniels

What's Next?

I've got several more non-fiction books in the works as part of The Natural Path series. *An Introduction to Herbalism* is out now. *Home and Cleaning Solutions*, and *Body and Skincare Solutions* will be coming soon.

Stay tuned, friends!

Willa Daniels

<u>Jen Flanagan Fiction Books</u>

Orca Cove Series:
Saltwater Cures
Uncharted Waters
Star Crossed (coming 2025)

Books in the Detective Malone Series:
Bad Company
Here I Go Again
Under Pressure

<u>Willa Daniels Non-Fiction Books</u>

Stand-alone books:
The Art of Living Seasonally

The Natural Path Series:
An Introduction to Herbalism
An Introduction to Soapmaking
Home and Cleaning Solutions (coming 2025)
Body and Skincare Solutions (coming 2025)

Willa Daniels

www.ingramcontent.com/pod-product-compliance
Lightning Source LLC
Chambersburg PA
CBHW060257030426
42335CB00014B/1735